In the Dark Woods

Written by Hawys Morgan

Illustrated by Marina Perez Luque

Collins

The moon lights up the woods.

Hear the fox bark.

Look up high in this oak.

Hush! Owls hoot.

Toads soak in the pool.

The air feels cool.

Look in the marsh.

Eels coil up in the weeds.

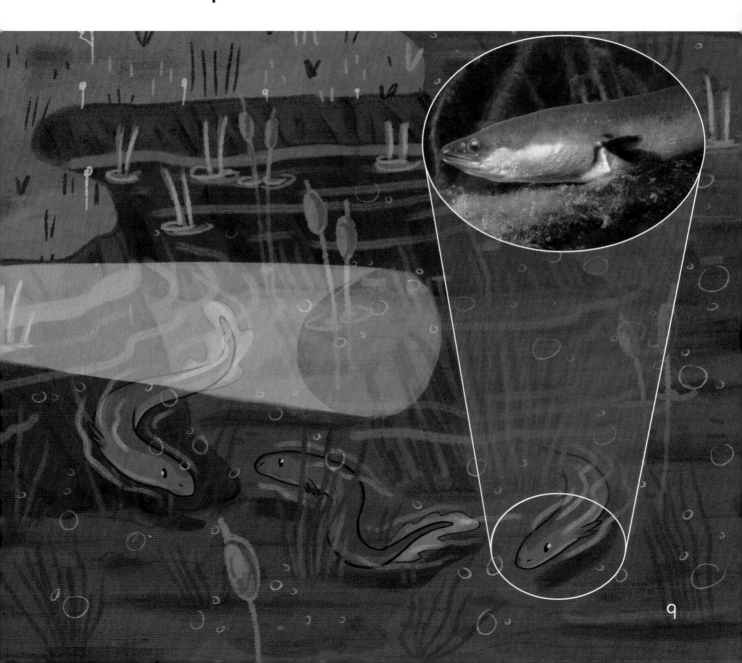

We see a herd.

We hear a moan.

hurt foot

11

Mum is a vet.

She cures the hoof.

The woods

After reading

Letters and Sounds: Phase 3

Word count: 60

Focus phonemes: /ee/ /igh/ /oa/ /oo/ /oo/ /ar/ /ur/ /ow/ /oi/ /ear/ /air/ /ure/ /er/ /or/

Common exception words: the, we, she

Curriculum links: Understanding the world

Early learning goals: Reading: read and understand simple sentences; use phonic knowledge to decode regular words and read them aloud accurately; read some common irregular words

Developing fluency

- Your child may enjoy hearing you read the book.
- Take turns to read a page with your child. Ensure they also read the labels. Encourage your child to read with a whisper to add to the atmosphere.

Phonic practice

- Focus on the words in which two or three letters make one sound.
- Turn to page 13. Point to **cures** and challenge your child to sound out and blend. Can they identify the three letters that make one sound? (*ure*)

Extending vocabulary

- Ask your child:
  - On page 9, what shape do the eels make? (*a coil*)
  - What else makes a coil shape? (e.g. *a snake, a snail's shell*)
  - On page 10, can you suggest a word that has a similar meaning to **herd**? (e.g. *group, crowd*)